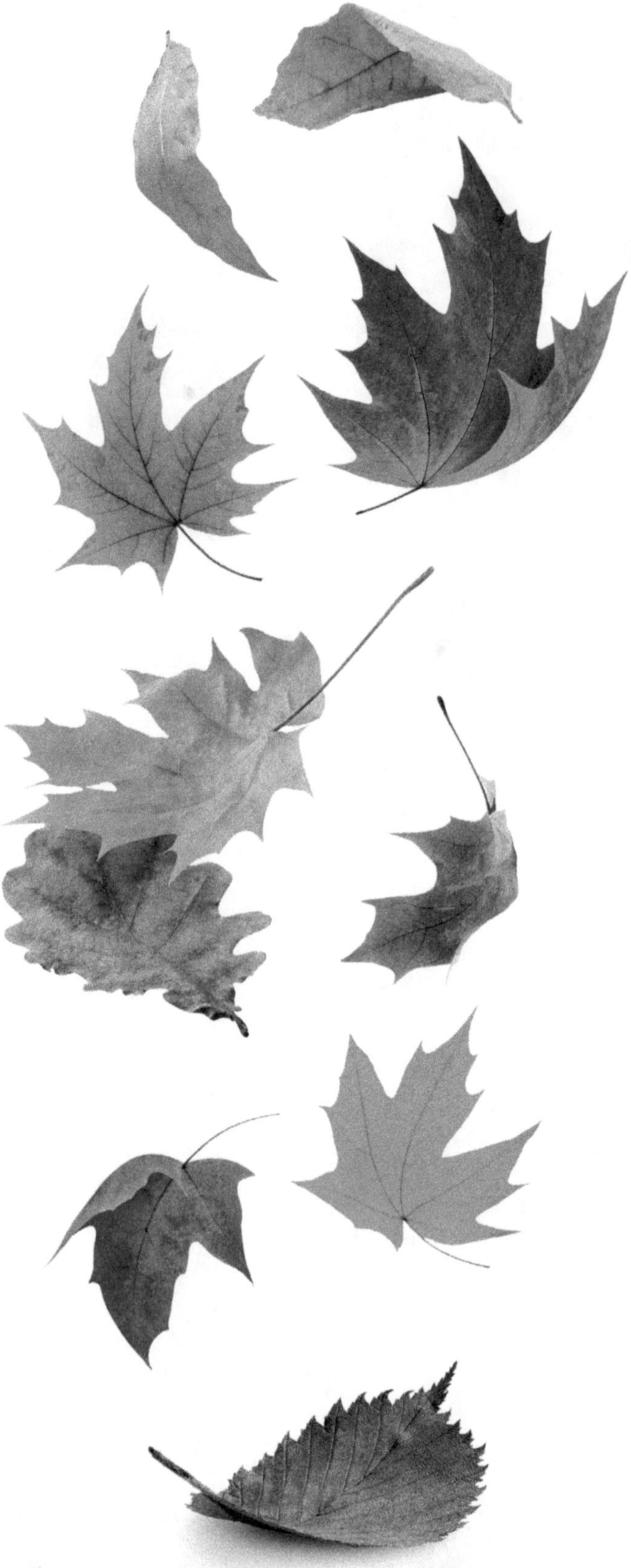

A Scattering of Leaves

Copyright © 2024 by R. Royce Perkins

All rights reserved.

ISBN 978-1-62806-419-3 (print | paperback)

Library of Congress Control Number 2024916548

Published by Salt Water Media
29 Broad Street, Suite 104
Berlin, MD 21811
www.saltwatermedia.com

Cover art via istockphoto.com with proper license

A Scattering of Leaves

R. Royce Perkins

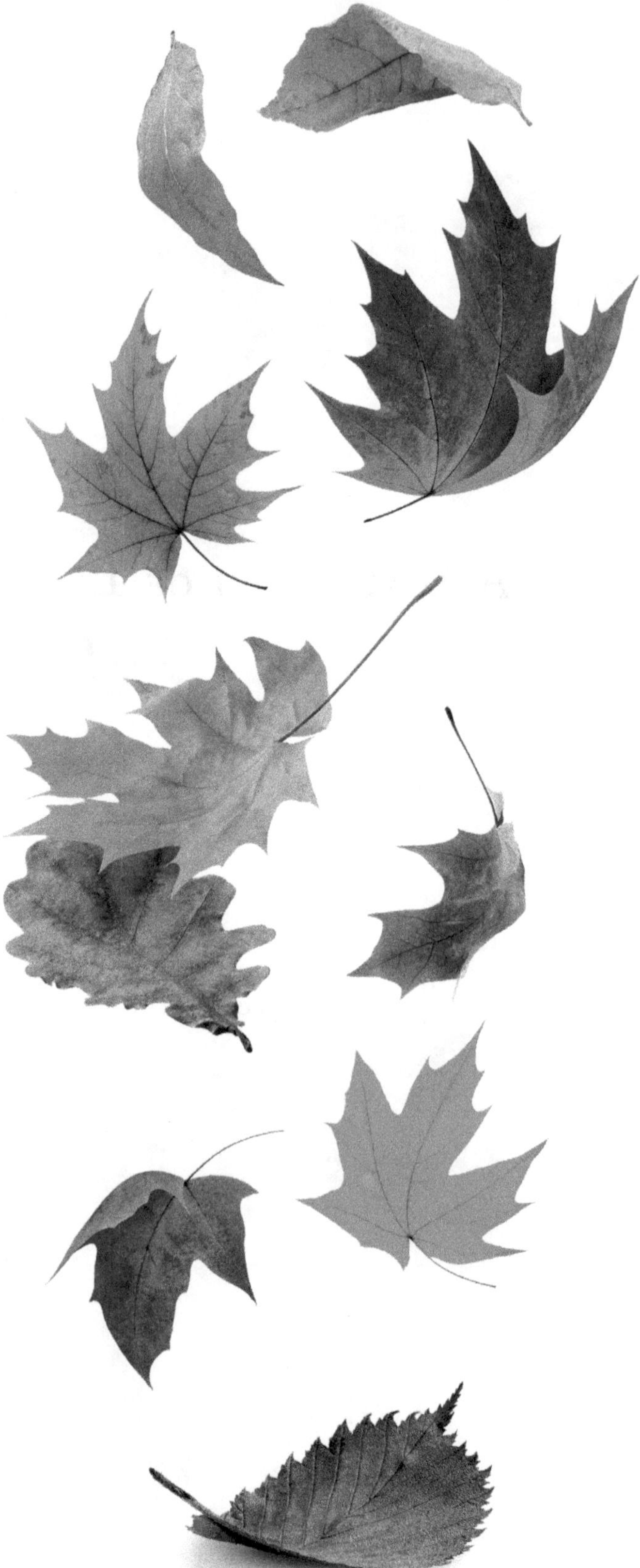

To Sandi

*Thank you for saving my life
and for always being there for me.*

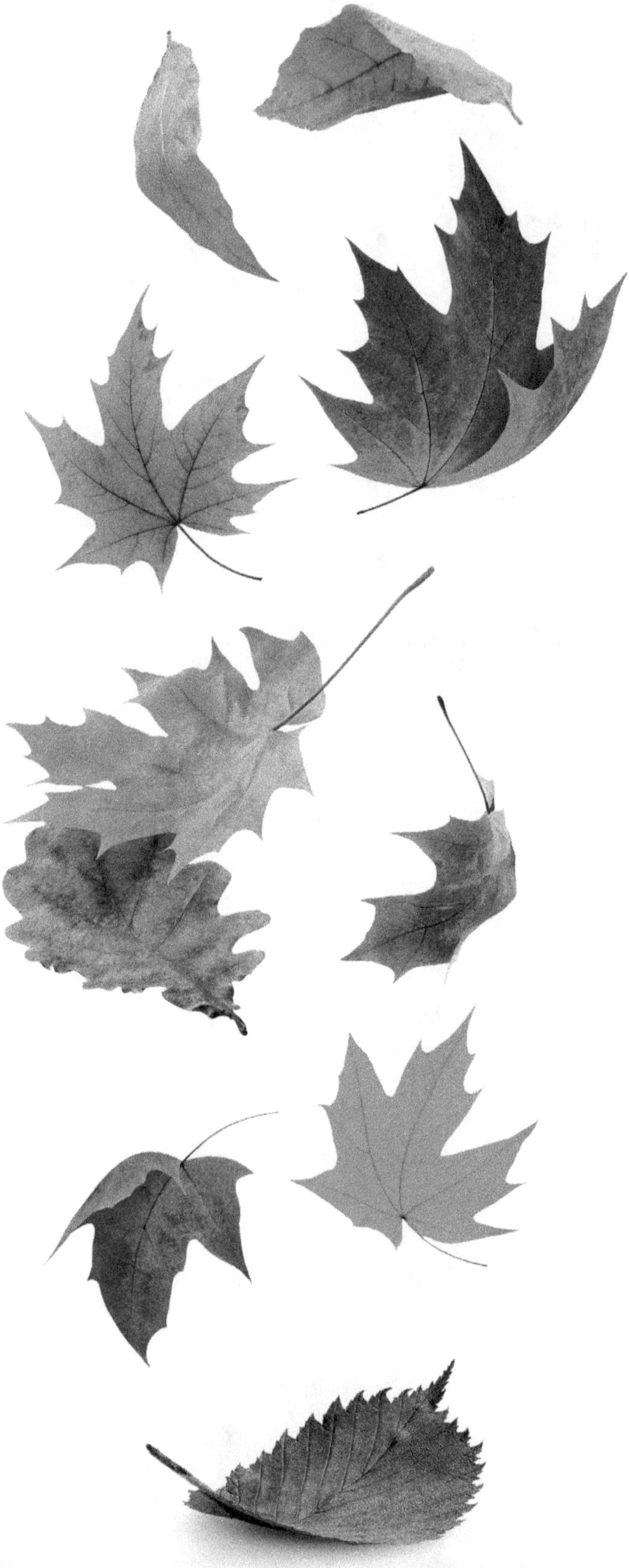

Acknowledgements

Many thanks to all my friends from Colonial High School and Facebook and beyond who encouraged me to get my poems published. (I won't name names because I don't want to leave someone out. You know who you are.) Thanks also to Stephanie Fowler and Andrew Heller at Salt Water Media who helped me through this process. You have helped me to realize a lifelong dream!

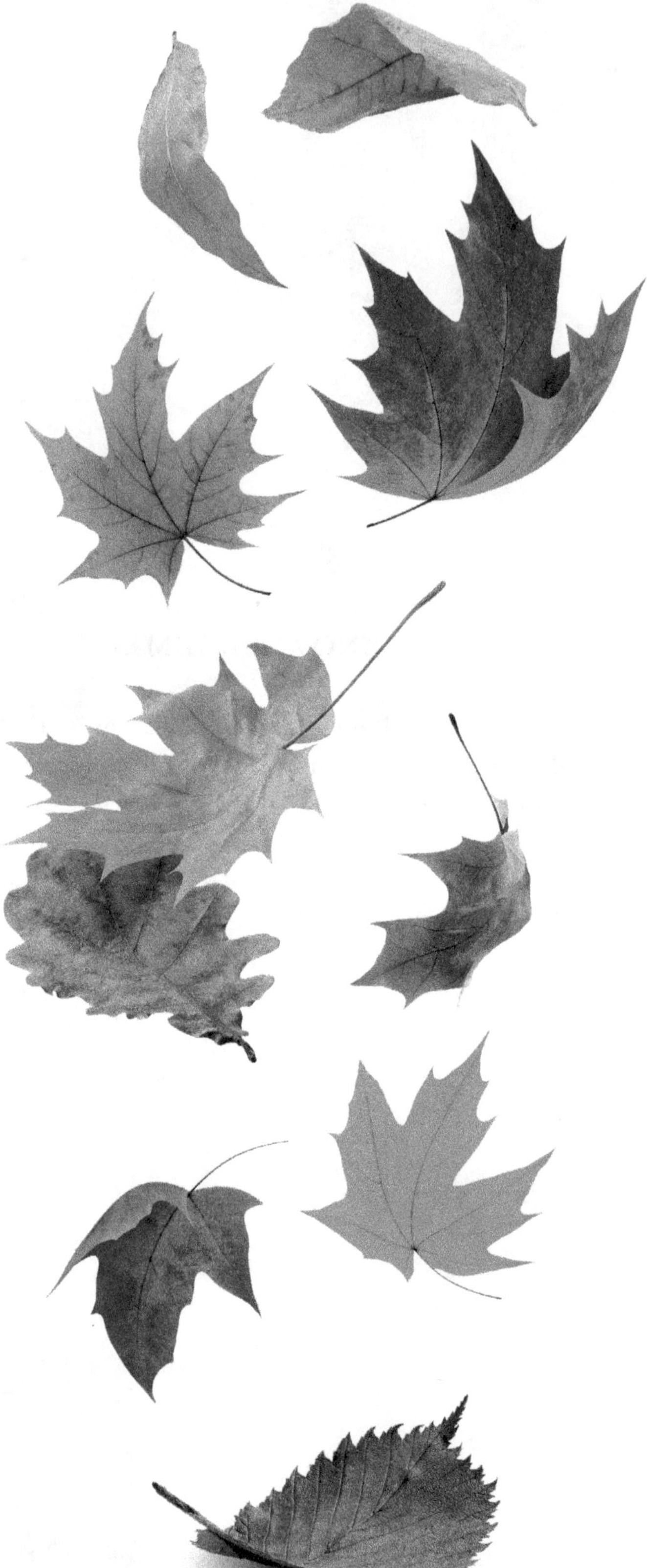

Foreword

I started writing poetry when I was in the Navy back in the 60's (that's 1960's). The first poem in this book is the first poem that I wrote back in those days. I got into the habit of needing to put pen to paper after I had been drinking, and this led to many things being written during what I call "my dark period". This period lasted a long time, because I continued to drink even after I got married to Sandi.

Eventually, I was able to kick the alcohol habit (with the help of God and the support of my wife) and began to see goodness and light where I had known only depression and darkness. As a result, my writings became more upbeat and introspective. I'll let you determine which one came from which period.

Although I enjoy writing, I realize that for me it is mainly a catharsis. When something happens to me or I see something memorable, I feel compelled to write about it. Some of my more introspective works come from memories of yesteryear that I can write about because the fog of angst and alcohol has been lifted.

I will be the first to admit that I am not a learned poet. Poetry by some of the greats—Whitman, Whittier, Plath, Frost, Sandburg and many others never fails to blow me away. I think Robert Frost is my favorite of all time. His "The Road Not Taken" and "Stopping by Woods on a Snowy Evening" still amaze me every time I read them. I find much poetry too difficult to understand, and to me that is not enjoyable. Some of these musings I have offered to you in this small volume of verse might veer into the difficult lane at times, but I blame that on the alcohol (those poems are very old).

I hope that you enjoy taking this journey with me. Perhaps you will find something that kindles a flame in your heart, or at least something that resonates with your emotions.

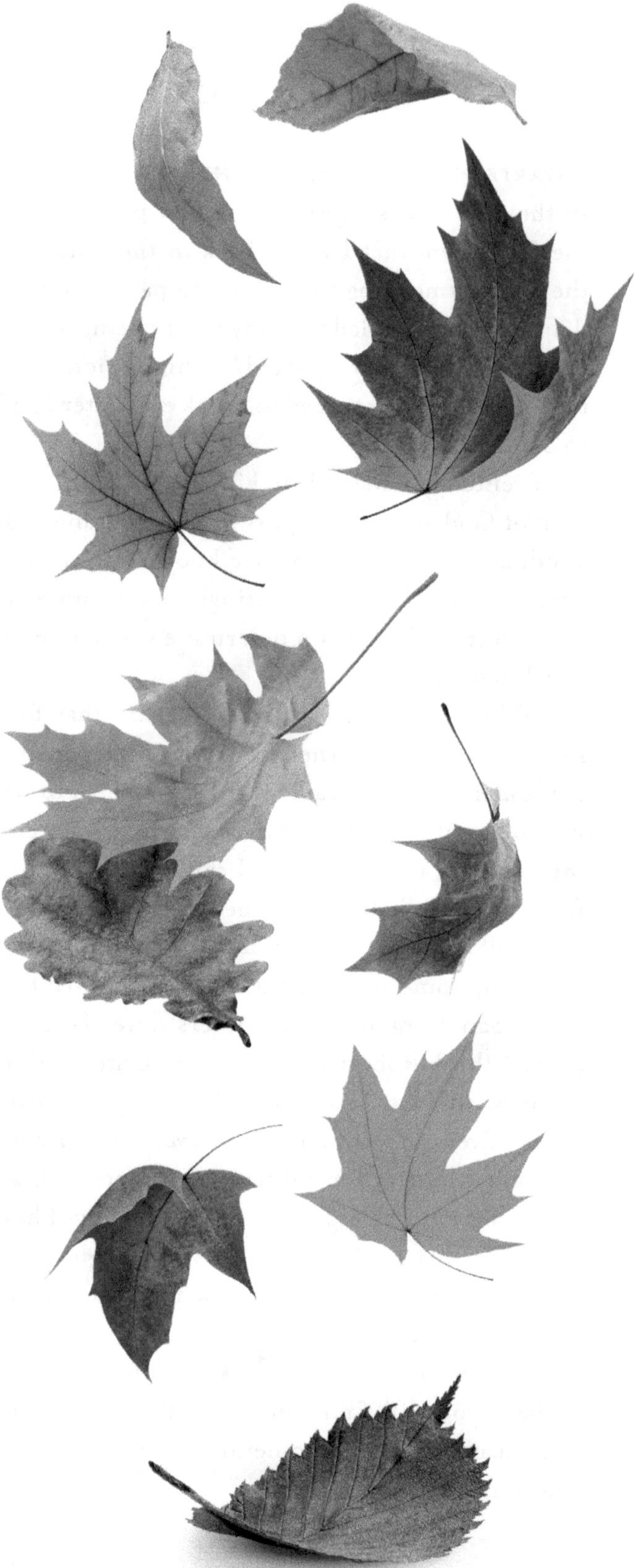

Contents

Song of the Pastel Sparrow 1

A Scattering of Leaves 5

Small Moments 6

Down by the River 7

A Degree of Understanding 9

A Highly Respected Institution 10

A Moment of Time Somewhere 11

Blind Dreams 12

Bring Me Death 13

Candle Flame 14

Candle Glow 14

Cheap Escape 15

Cold Train Gone 16

Country Fair 17

Destiny 18

Dreams 19

Early One Morning 20

Face at the Window 21

Final Laugh 22

Final Thoughts 23

Forver Ila Fern 24

Goodbye to Someone 25

Heartache	26
Journeys	28
Lonely	29
Looking Back From the Light	30
Morning Breaks	31
Night Bird	32
Ode to B.D.	33
Ode to Other Times	34
Old Friends	35
On Rainy Days	36
On the Shores of Lake Keowee	38
Other Times of Sorrow	39
Plea	40
Questioning Love	41
Sailing an Endless Sea	42
Sky at Night	43
Softly Revealed	44
Someone's Epitaph	45
Song Journey	46
Store-Bought Sentiment	47
Summer Meadows	48
Sunday Close to You	49
The Awakening	50

The Game	52
The Gate	53
The Glass	55
The Hunt	56
The Park	58
The Smiling Executioner	59
Through an Amber Glass	61
Time and Memories	62
Time, Roads, Circles	63
Tonight	64
Truth	65
Walls	66
Within	68
You	69
My Heart Was Fallow Ground	70
This Stormy Sea	72
Sandi	74
Serenity	75
About the Author	77

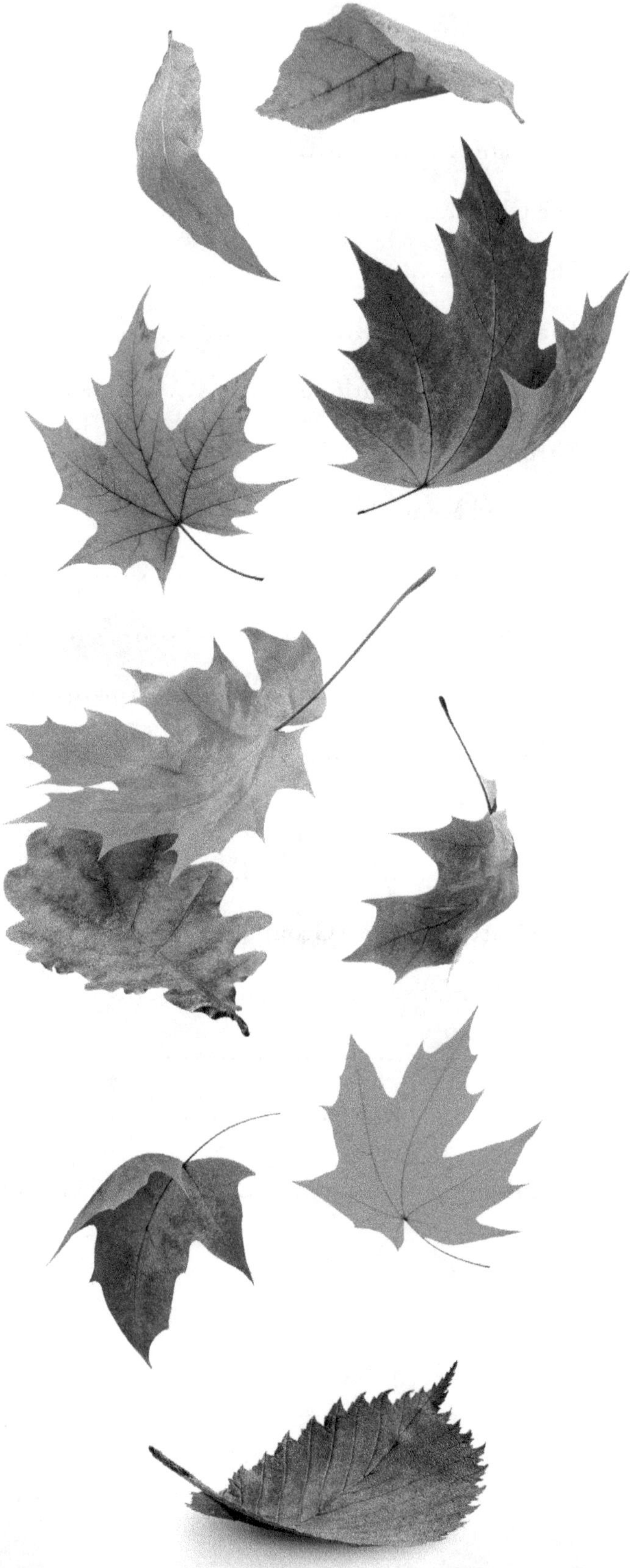

Song of the Pastel Sparrow

through the gentle morning
rains
the pastel sparrow wings,
the golden clouds that
follow make him sparkle;
inside your mind you
see him bright,
but your mirrored eyes
are glazed
they are hindered by
the haze
they have wandered
far too long
they see nothing
but a song
though the midnight with
its darkness brings
a vision.

he brings with him
the laughter wine
the sunshine of the day,
all the flowers in
the meadow lay
a-sleeping;
quench your thirst
with nectar dreams,
your mind shall fly
away
let his wings
sing yesterday
as you dance upon
the sky
and the world spins
slowly by

bright lights of
reality explode
within you.

as the luminescent
dewdrops fade into
the autumn air
all the shadows of
the present seem
to shroud you;
ethereal wing beats of
the soul
split the air around
your ears
as they brush away
your tears
and the sparrow
takes to flight
in the brightness
of the night
with me upon his
back the sunrise
fading.

the wind now sends
him reeling through
untravelled blissfulness
where the love that
binds the heart is
disappearing;
unfolding petals
beckon to his
wavering desire
but tomorrow sends
him higher
out of reach of
all the skies

untouched by the
many lies
even though the
truths he believes
in are
forgotten.

over crystal hills
of day
and dark meadows of
the night
the rising sun that
is now so close
behind him
touches his wings
with amber-gold
before he fades
from sight
a fugitive from
the light
a prisoner of
your dreams
a phantom so he
seems
as he rests within
your soul until
you need him.

but now the sparrow's
night is gone
silently he leaves
you just
a-waking;
and stolen with
him a part of you
a corner of your
mind

that leaves you
more than blind
without a voice
to say
that you died
before the day
and you know that
somewhere peaceful
he lies
sleeping.

A Scattering of Leaves

Autumn skies of wonder
So clear and deeply blue,
Strong and yet so fragile
With Winter in the wings.

Trudging through the fallen leaves
Such a noise it makes,
The clattering and the scattering
Fall's music that I love.

And cars that pass by quickly
Create chaos in their wake,
The dancing swirls of color
Take flight and touch my face.

I have seen so many years
These Autumns come and go,
But the scattering of the leaves
Is forever in my heart.

Small Moments

I live my life in fragments of time,
Each moment begifted is truly sublime.
I collect them all and toss them away
And hope more are coming that I can make stay.

We all have allotments of time we can spend,
Some use them wisely, knowing they may soon end.
And some of us squander the moments we're sent,
We wallow in anguish when they are all spent.

No fortune will purchase not one single day,
Nor second, nor minute could we but repay
For we saw no reason to treasure them so,
We frittered and wasted, while knowing they'd go.

So each moment is special, it's like an old friend,
To be treated with kindness as if it were kin,
It won't last forever, and soon it is gone,
With the end of the night comes the breaking of dawn.

Down by the River

Long days of summer,
The sun takes its toll.
Along the dirt road as the
Dust devils roll.
But the cool, clear water
Is calling to me, I know
Down by the river
Where the cottonwood grows.

Autumn's approaching,
With its leaves all ablaze.
Some fire and some copper,
Some pumpkin, some maize.
Soon winter will be here,
And the land will be froze'
Down by the river,
Where the cottonwood grows.

Down the long highway
My boot heels have trod.
I looked for an answer,
And finally found God.
My friends are all scattered,
Like shadows on snow
Down by the river,
Where the cottonwood grows.

And now I've come
To the end of my days.
My life was a journey
In so many ways.
Now I'll rest when I'm weary
And sleep when it snows
Down by the river
Where the cottonwood grows.

And when you come visit,
The winds will be still
As you sit in the sunshine
At the base of the hill.
I will speak to you softly,
So that you'll finally know
 We're all down by the river
Where the cottonwood grows.

A Degree of Understanding

Lo, lest the petal fall
Upon the frozen land so
Still
And never be heard within
Its hour; all creation
Stands to hear
The moment of a final death,
Caught between the birth
And death of always.
Knowing you are near,
We stand beside the
Moment
And look into ourselves.

A Highly Respected Institution

Mausoleum of madness,
Near painful cacophony of
Tears and laughter, sounds
That only bleed, washed
Away by numbed fingers;
Confusion in a house of mirrors,
Reflections distorted by
Perception, interpretations
In error.
Asylum of paranoia,
Shelter for the exorcism
Of soul from self;
Intricate meaningless patterns
Of shadows and light, mercurial
Shifts of prevailing winds
And doldrums;
Undercurrent of sadness,
Eddies of desire, unfeeling
Hands that grasp and never
Touch, remain attached to
The bodies that remain
Within the walls.

A Moment of Time Somewhere

Here upon the midnight silence,
Come the waves that shatter shore,
To touch the sands streaked with silver
And then are gone forevermore.

Yet we remain to feel the sadness,
Of friends, like waves, forever gone;
The moon looks on as frail men plunder
Precious moments before the sun.

A tear, a laugh, a cherished story,
Some small remembrance cast about;
A tale of all the tarnished glory
And how the then became the now.

In silence then again we part,
To seek the paths that life unfolds,
In memory only, youth eternal,
Like faded pages, we all grow old.

Blind Dreams

Bring me a dream, or buy me a rainbow
Tell me a secret or two.
Pick me a flower, find me a forest
Paint me a sky softly blue.

Climb me a mountain, sail me an ocean,
Walk me a valley so green.
Save me a sunset, cloud me with wonder,
Tell me the things you have seen.

Kiss me soft a summer sky
Chill me with Winter snow,
Warm me with a high-tide fire,
Tell me the things that you know.

Touch me with the golden sunshine
And know me as I am,
I've never known the world outside,
I've only touched your hand.

Paint the pines upon my senses,
Tell me they are real.
Give to me their cool reflection,
Does it hurt me just to feel?

Bring Me Death

Will there never be an end,
Out of the darkness must you follow me?
Only if there were someone
To conquer you
And make me free

Given that I am just a man,
A weakened soldier in the field
Pity me when I reach out
For what I see
That isn't real

And so denied I stand alone
To scoff the name that you assume
There is no other cloak I own
My life is all,
This tranquil room

Call my name, I'm sure you must
Hold my hand, steal my breath
And all alone we are but dust,
I'll have no tomorrows
Give me death.

Candle Flame

This flame that burns
So brightly
Must someday touch the dark.

Candle Glow

Alone in the night,
Soul smoke
On the wind.

Cheap Escape

Waxen figures move,
Dispensing sorrow casually
For promise of eternity
And bartering the misery
To hapless souls who never
Slake their thirst.

Lonely eyes that stare
Through thunder lights
And neon sounds,
As glasses touch their
Lips to drown
The hundred shades of
Gray and brown,
Like waves so restless
In the smoky air.

Pain misplaced,
The clink of bottles a
Sound of chimes,
Distant laughter at
The pass of time,
And somewhere lost
Amidst the din
A teardrop falls and
Shatters silently.

As the lights go up
And the music fades,
On empty smiles
And promises made,
The souls will slowly
Find their way
To wrap the darkness
Like a shroud
And steal into the
Night.

Cold Train Gone

Drive wheels sing a symphony
Along the silver rails
Westbound freight that sings to me
The music never fails

My heart and all my dreams
In yellow boxcars run
And find me ever far from here
When all the day is done

Moon on midnight steel rails shine
Like memories of friends
Sounds of outbound misery
Whistle moaning, without end

Long into the darkness ride
And take away the pain
Somehow fading in the night
Some lonesome sad refrain

And as I stand and watch you go
My heart shall e'er take wing
Like magic in a field of dark
You're gone and still you sing.

Country Fair

Catch the stallion in the
Madness carnival on the magic carousel
Flying wild and free,
Riding all alone in
The neon midnight.

Cotton candy dreams that are
Spun with silver,
Candy apple moments frozen in
Time.

Try your luck, take a chance,
Just a nickel for your soul;
Win a doll and be proud,
Or in debt, makes no difference.

Ferris wheel that slides into the void,
Screams from the past,
Spinning around eternity,
A prize-winning pie.

Sunday evening, the fair
Is closing. People drifting
Away with backs turned
And heads bowed,
Just about the end of day,
Just about the end of time.

Destiny

Ghosts in a crowd
Mock me in silence,
A burden to be
Carried in the light,
Too heavy to bear.
Each step takes me
Away from my heart,
To the pyre
Where I throw myself.
Thoughts that leap
Like flame on brass,
Warm me in the cold
And fill the dark
With light.
In time, in time,
The trips grow longer,
And I am weary
Like death.
Yet still I try to set my feet
Upon that darkened road,
But soon
I will make the journey
No more.

Dreams

Somewhere
There is a place
Where midnight falls like
Silk upon the snow,
And morning breaks in colored shards
That lay upon the land
Like interrupted dreams.

Early One Morning

Dewdrop sparkles, emerald swords,
Tiny prisms, points of fire
Softly touching all the earth
Vermilion threads, sapphire

Morning mists like kittens play,
Rolling softly in the air
Comforter of down, so light
Steals into the morning's lair

Birds awaken, greet the day
Gentle songs, night is past
Amber, gold, flecks of silver
Pastel crimson, sun at last.

Face at the Window

Cold, rain that fails
To cleanse and wash away the
Thoughts I am having,
Lost within myself
I gaze for a moment
At a window high above
And there, distorted by
The rivulets and the
Yellow aged glass
A face, gazing back at me;
Haunting, I cannot
Clearly see the eyes
Of this specter
That sits and stares at
The crowded street below.
What are the thoughts?
Are they of longing?
Does this specter wish to
Be among his own kind
Or is that far away in his
Past?
Only a moment I reflect,
For I am swept up in the
Tide and move on.

Final Laugh

Oh darkness, in your blasphemy
Could still my heart and freeze these limbs,
Torn asunder from a world familiar,
Cast upon an unknown shore.

Without shield to face the mourning,
Veils are drawn to hide the smiles,
Laughing as the grave is dug
A final resting, evermore.

Then laughter from the tomb reverberates,
Round about the sacred soil,
For I have reached my destination,
A peaceful resting, evermore.

Final Thoughts

This struggle ending,
Time not a friend,
The wind plays no music
The fire has lost
Its warmth.
Gray is the color
Of the shroud
Over us all.

There is silence in the tunnel,
Darkness in the carnival
That preys upon the soul.

If there is a soul.

Falling curtain,
The play is over now,
The actors gone from
The empty stage.

Forever Ila Fern

Softly beats somewhere a song
Of all your life;
Some calliope speaking, and
Telling us the stories
Of your life
And your heart;

All our photographs will fade
In time, but we will always
Have the song.

Somewhere in the void,
You ride the wind
Across an ocean, rolling
Under night skies, lit by
Moonlight silver on the waves,
To gaze upon castles on
A foreign shore,
To see the sun rise
Forever,
To touch the pink of
Sunsets,
To be one
With God;

We miss you so, Mother, friend and
companion. We miss your laughter
and your way of looking at life.
We miss most of all your positive
ways and quickness of smiles.

Someday, we will all
Be together again,
And our song will
Touch
The stars.

Goodbye to Someone

Through the fields of flowers
We found our way,
Light were our steps, lest we
Stumble, lose our way,
Light was our touch, lest we
Suddenly need someone
To guide us;

Amidst the rainbow madness
With abandon we ran free,
Time was nothing to us,
We were alone and free,
Cares to the wind, for
We needed no one
To guide us;

Alone I stand here in
The fading colors,
As thunderstorms pass through
To blend these colors,
Passions spent, that bring
To mind the need for
Someone to guide us.

Heartache

You think that it's not true
But then, you would
Be wrong,
Heartache isn't just a word
That you hear in a song.

The pain is so very real
And it goes
On and on
Heartache isn't just a word
That you hear in a song.

The heavy feeling weighs you down
And keeps you
Feeling low
Until you wonder just how far
Into the dark you'll go.

Will you ever see the light again?
Will the pain
Soon go away?
But memories, like poltergeists
Keep the light at bay.

"Enough", you cry, "please take
These woes and from
This realm depart;
I've had my share of sorrow
In my frail and hurting heart".

As time goes by
You feel the warmth from the
Life-preserving sun;
Bit by bit you live again
But it's never really done.

For the rest of time, in many ways,
You're reminded
Of the pain.
But now you have the warming sun
And sadness cannot reign.

Journey

Blackness,
Darkness never ending
Swirling past my eyes,
Bursting into ebony rainbows
Flowing through my being;
Falling gently,
Currents carry me
Only down, further
Down into the
Depths, the Stygian
Absence of light;
Clouds of death, rolling
Tumbling flashes of
Phosphorescent Nubian
Emptiness, shearing
The night without
Lighting the way;
Fear of opening my eyes,
What would I discover
But the crushing burden
Of the untold horrors
That await me;
Fury building to a
Climax, crashing,
Thrusting me down,
Ever down,
Maniacal laughter as
I finally am ground
Into the pitch
Oh God
Have I reached the bottom?

Lonely

A flower
In a field of stones,

A single firefly on
a summer's night;

Lighthouse on a
rocky shore,

Star of brightness
In the Stygian dark;

The ragpicker shuffles
down the empty street
and fades into the mist.

Looking Back from the Light

May the night take me in
One shade beyond indigo,
And the darkness that I know
Enshroud me in its folds.

Oh, night! Beast without eyes,
That seeks me out by day,
And looks in wonder when I say
"Why have you tarried so"?

This ebony, let it comfort me,
And hold me small and warm,
And keep me safe from harm,
Dark covers soft to touch.

Farewell, companion of the dreams
That brought solace, treasured dear,
And kept a memory held so near,
As the day begins its reign.

Morning Breaks

Morning paints the golden pines
And fills the air with song
Hopes and dreams awaken now
To face the newborn dawn

The day awaits, and beckons me
To open wide my eyes.
To see the pastel colors
That are wrapped around the skies.

A tattered fog lies sleepily
Upon the forest floor.
A doe takes tiny halting steps
As she carefully explores.

From my highest window
I gaze upon the scene.
In awe of all the beauty there,
In pink and gold and green.

I hold this picture in my heart
As I begin my day.
For I will find some comfort there,
As travails come my way.

Night Bird

Alone again,
And I hear the night bird's call
That echoes through the emptiness
And conjures up the demons of the
Mind.
They dance and taunt me
Until I am in tears,
Their laughter ringing through
The darkness.

Alone again,
I hear not the night bird's cry
For companionship to make
Him whole.

His soul is filled and I
Am still awake and still
Alone again.

Ode to B.D.

Hail the young troubadour,
Unpolished diamond who
Changed my dreams
And all my visions,
Carry me to the light.
Through your eyes
I learned the truth
And found the road
To be long and winding
And sometimes lonely.
Words that come so
Easily to you are born
To me in agony, ripped
From me like a
Beating heart.
If only I could see the lights
Of the city and feel the bite
Of northern winds,
And find some girl in
The north country.
The original vagabond,
I steal words that I cannot repay,
Words that fit you like
A suit of armor;
In your castle strong,
Beyond ramparts I will
Never climb, I gaze
At you.
Somehow,
If only our words and music
Could find each other...
Strange dreams, I will admit;
In these early hours
Before dawn....
You've been there too,
I know.

Ode to Other Times

The softest touch of a whisper
Lingers yet in my drowsy mind,
Sweet memories
Of rolling meadows
With golden rivers
Flowing in the lazy sunshine,
A world where love
And peace
Are the
Bread and wine.
As all emotions go
Cascading
Down the cliffs
Of forgetfulness,
To burst into
Shimmering spray,
The falling drops
Will cleanse my soul.
I drink of the
Wandering cup,
My travels reflected
In pastel rainbows
And the wind.
Someday, while
There is yet sunshine,
I may pass through
Again.

Old Friends

You and I, against the world…
Lord, we fought the battles,
The demons within and
The fools outside,
Numbered in the millions.

Only our thoughts keep us tethered
To our expectations,
And they make us laugh, and cry;
Tears and laughter in symphony.

The years keep rolling on,
The Ferris wheel turns,
The calliope plays
And we walk together
Facing the sun.

On Rainy Days

The weather has taken a turn
for the worse, they say,
But oh, how I look forward
to a gray and rainy day.

The world becomes still
as it seeks a dry shelter,
And the raindrops run rampant
hither and yon, helter-skelter.

And I in my cave
with pen in my hand,
Take comfort in delaying
all my best-laid plans.

For these are the days
that I cherish above all,
When I reflect on my life
and I begin to recall

All the moments in time
that in my heart reside,
The ones that have shaped me,
like an ongoing tide.

I wander in words that
resemble my thoughts,
And carefully choose them,
so painfully sought.

The results make me lighter,
unburdening my load,
And I continue unhindered,
Down a scarce-travelled road.

And my world seems much brighter,
even though there is gloom,
As I contemplate raindrops
While safe in my room.

On the Shores of Lake Keowee

Sultry days in the Cherokee Hills
We gathered together as old friends will.
For the Rendezvous in '23,
On the shores of Lake Keowee

Many a tale was told in fun,
Many a yarn was embellished, then spun.
Laughter was a common sound,
With friendship as the common ground

With lazy summer days to spend
We hoped that they would never end.
While most just sat and reminisced,
And remembered times that we all missed.

For our journeys soon will reach an end
And now it seems that trusted friends,
Are valued highly, more than gold
And even more, as we grow old.

In many ways we all were blessed,
The hugs and laughter said it best.
And now the miles again divide
As we are spread so far and wide.

And though we all did travel home,
We knew that we were not alone.
We carry with us this history,
Of our sweet time on Lake Keowee.

Other Times of Sorrow

Do not despair,
My love,
There are times for you
When you can embrace
Your dreams, fields of
Sun and flowers of tomorrow;
Too much time, too much time
For other times of sorrow.

Fear not the night,
My love,
For it is but a quilt
Of solitude, a private
Cloak that you can wear
That no one else can borrow;
Time enough, time enough
For other times of sorrow.

Play the blues,
My love,
Diversions on the road,
Footsteps form the light,
They lead you to the dawn
And you will see tomorrow;
The time is now, the time is now
For other times of sorrow.

Plea

I have no place to go,
And I thought that you could help,
To rearrange my thoughts of life
And give direction to
This road I travel down,
That I don't really know,
And yet I meet with false bravado
Every day;
And yet I realize you have yourself
To care for,
And you have your own roads
To travel,
So I ask only in a whisper,
Help me find myself.

Questioning Love

Only moments that are fleeting
In the future, in the past
We grasp what we are given
For we know in cannot last

Fewer seconds in the knowing
Fewer minutes than the years
Only hours that are passing
Just a touch away from tears

Finally knowing that forever
Is to us a state of mind
In the searching is the answer
For we know what we will find

Always falling, never standing
As we try to walk alone
We are bound by all our weakness
And the things we should have done

There is never just one answer
For there is one question more
Are we sailing on the ocean
Are we dying on the shore?

Are we sailing on the ocean
Are we dying on the shore?

Sailing an Endless Sea

As the waves crash upon the shore,
And the moon paints silver upon the sea,
I breathe in the smell of salt and storms,
There is where I always wish to be.

For in my mind I sail the oceans,
'Til the storms of life force me to the land,
Biding my time, my love unrequited,
My heart on the ocean, my feet in the sand.

I remember midnights black and cold uncaring,
The sea like a mirror save for the churning wake,
No land in sight on a perfect night,
I am filled with awe with each breath I take.

The stars and the moon both light the way,
Beacons on an endless journey they shine.
One beholds them with a sense of wonder,
Standing guard 'til the end of time.

There seemed to be a sense of freedom,
This forever journey, upon a boundless sea,
As water and sky flow darkly by,
There's no one left on earth but me.

And I stand alone, cold and proud,
Weary, yet vigilant still.
Soon enough will be time for rest,
My duties all fulfilled.

This is a time I revisit often,
As the years erase my youth,
For on those waters so far behind me,
I finally learned to see the truth.

Sky at Night

Behold this firmament
Shot with silver, laced with grey
Ebon wisps all turned about,
The blue
Has yet to fade away

Is there heaven as close as this,
Fragile web, nightly veil?
To guide a soul who wanders there
Flicker, shadows
On the trail

Or does the storm assume command,
Melting canvas into black,
For souls adrift along the road,
It means
For them no turning back.

Softly Revealed

As the light is cast down upon me,
So does the truth touch me.
A light in the darkness,
A gate in the fence,
A clearing in the forest that has seen
Only shadow.
It finds us here unbelieving,
Unwilling to see that what we
Know may upset the
Delicate balance,
And wash away our masks.

Someone's Epitaph

Death,
Bring to me the
Peace of no more
Pain.
No more wondering,
No more guilt.
Dark dove,
Eternal steed, fly away,
I've finally let
My burden fall.

Song Journey

Sometimes when I'm dreaming long,
Into the night there comes a song
And you come sailing back to me
Across the sea of memories
To hold me until the night has passed.

Through the clouds as my soul wings,
To hear a thousand voices sing
I'm caught up in my reverie
For you're the one I long to see
And share the night that is fading fast.

In meadows here I watch the flowers,
And while the sun does trace the hours
My thoughts of you keep turning 'round
As in the distance there comes a sound
Of the thunder long before the storm.

Raindrops silver in the light,
That soon will shroud the day from night
I send my heart to journey long
I send to you this lonely song
Perhaps it may just help to keep you warm.

Store-Bought Sentiment

Speak to me in phrases sweet
Like a half-dollar
Drugstore card.
Promises like parasols,
That fly away on
A windy day.
Cloud castles, changing
Into dream prisons
Where I lay by the winter fire.
Empty lines of love,
You can sign and
Forget.
Send them with flowers
And smile,
As you lay by the winter fire
And wonder
Where is the truth?
One tender moment,
Borne on a paper heart,
Becomes the kindling
For the fire,
And the thoughts, like smoke,
Disappear into
The wind.

Summer Meadows

All the flowers soft and
Glorious in rainbow confusion,
These wondrous meadows
Pastel fantasies that ripple
And flow with the breeze;
Infinite colours, and shades that
Rival the azure sky, yet
Blend together as feathers on
The wing of a dove;
Dragonflies whirring iridescent in
The warm air, gossamer wings
That glint and reflect the honey
Sun;
Cool and fragrant touches of wind,
Soothing the soul, calming;
Lazy buzz of grasshoppers lend
A melody to the symphony of
Wind and flowers;

Days of summer meadows,
Endless days of summer love.

Sunday Close to You

Such an easy kind of feeling,
On a Sunday afternoon,
And I knew that as with all things,
It would end too soon.

There comes a time for leaving,
As we say our own good-byes
To our own thoughts and our secrets,
But still I wonder why...

Does there have to be a sunset,
And why does it come so soon,
Why can't it be forever
Just a Sunday afternoon?

The Awakening

Say farewell to winter
In all its browns and grays,
And welcome in the splendor
Of Spring's new glorious days

The birds are so excited
As sunlight warms their wings,
They give voice to their ebullience
Through all the songs they sing.

The bees are busy buzzing
Around the early flowers,
Tireless workers in the sun
And through the April showers.

Though the daffodils have faded
The dogwoods are in bloom,
And soon wisteria will climb on high
In lavender festoons.

The trees are trying on
Their brand-new emerald cloaks,
They soon will fill the forest,
The maples, elms and oaks.

The sky is clean and cloudless
And such a crystal blue,
So deep and bright its color
Almost a purple hue.

The stately pines stand tall and proud
And whisper in the wind,
Like reeds along a riverbank
They dance and sway and bend.

There is no place for sadness
In this peaceful, awesome place,
As Spring awakens joyfully
And puts on a smiling face.

I wonder as I stand here
Will I see this time again?
And I remember all the years
And the places I have been.

There is no place that can compare
With this paradise on earth,
And once again I gaze upon
This beautiful re-birth.

The Game

Here are we again,
Willows by the river,
Fires in the city,
Poets in a line
Like soldiers.
Thoughts all jumbled
Like a puzzle in a box,
Dancing flames warm
The eyes
But not the heart.

Players in a game that never ends
Like winds across the plains,
Clouds across the sky,
Never resting.
Knowing not why, but
Rushing forth to meet
The day, abandoning
Our secret night fortress,
Standing small in the sun,
Prepared to play
The game.

The Gate

I stood there and gazed at the path, that appeared
 to have no end in sight, and seemed exciting to me
then. I travelled leisurely, and squandered steps here and
there, but I laughed and thought of those who
counted their steps and felt them to be foolish. At times, when the
light was right, and it may have been like a mirage, but I
could almost see a gate in the long fence.

It became a long, hard road that seemed to
take forever, and yet was over in the blink of an eye.
I know not why I was blessed so much, and how
I journeyed so long. Many friends that I remember,
were scattered in the dust long before, yet I was to set one foot
in front of the other, as days turned into years. And
as I looked to the horizon, and stared toward the future,
I saw it. There it was, far away, the gate in the long fence.

I saw the sea, and came to love her, yet she put me upon
the shore. I came to rest in the smaller hills, where the
trees are green and gold,
where the vines in spring are lavender, and where the leaves
finally can grow old. Sometimes in the morning mist,
I can barely see the trees, grey shadows, sentinels in
the clouds. And yet, there it is, not as far away in the fog
as it was before, the gate in the long fence.

And now my feet are weary, my boots worn from the
miles, my eyes
tired, my face weathered and beaten. I lean upon the
fence for support,
and falter in my step. The gate is there in front of me,
open a bit, expectantly.

I know that I am ready to swing it wide, and wander in, yet I fear that moment.

I turn to look back down the path, and all those who I have known have turned their eyes away from me, and seem not to know me.

This final part of my journey will be mine alone to take. I smile, and wave, and walk slowly through the gate.

The Glass

Crystal, fragile though it seems,
Reflects our thoughts and fantasies,
Amber in the evening sun,
Clear in the morning light.

Easily broken, brittle dreams,
Filled with sadness,
Or empty upon the shelf
And touched only by dust.

The Hunt

Early fall, the air so crisp
It crackles when words are spoken
Even in a whisper, for the woods
Are dark primeval.
Sky so clear you can touch the stars
As they trace their silver paths.
Dark as pitch the trail ahead,
Lit only by the heavens' splendor.
Tales are spun until the dawn
Creeps in on shades of gray.
Forget the fire that bound us close,
For the hunt still lies ahead.

And now we sit with thoughts unspoken,
As the forest reveals its secrets.
Behold the dawn, as it enters shyly
To spread its golden light
And find us here.

So quietly, he steals upon us,
Quivering tread on the forest floor;
This moment cannot last forever,
For we have come here to
Deal him death.

Quickly turning, the silence is broken
By the sound of a cannon,
Shattering forever this solitude.

And the trophy was within our grasp.

Only then did something leave me;
As his blood poured slowly forth,
A part of me died and
Lay there red upon the autumn leaves.

The sounds of joy were strangled
In me.

Here lies the prize! See what we have done!
See his life pour out,
Gone forever 'neath the morning sky.

Gone forever except to haunt me in the night.

The Park

Honey sun, warm
Cotton balls tumble across the sky
Winged song simplicity;

Ancient dreamer, lost
In yesterdays;

New life gamboling,
Laughter that fades
And rises, swells and
Recedes, waves breaking
Upon tenuous shores;
Burnished by youth,
Alive with careless wonder,
They pass before the gaze

Of the hoary spectator;

Solitary, eyes that dimly
See through ages' dust,
This anachronism drifts
Motionless in memories;
The cracked and weathered visage
Regales in silent mirth
With eyes that clearly see
A long-ago picture,
Honey sun, warm...

The Smiling Executioner

Dirty alleyways,
Pale forgotten figures that
May or may not come
To life
When the sun breaks
Through the rusty
Air
And brings the warmth
To the cold dead bodies,
Some stirring,
Some peaceful and
Sleeping forever, remembered
Only as a place in line.

Footsteps, sounding hollow
In a concrete canyon,
Ticks of time that
To some are a beginning
And to others are
Only a background,
A façade, a memory
Of the time when
They could walk.

Cold and crawling,
The mindless, soulless
Bodies converge upon the
Trough to slake their thirst
And to forget how they
Arrived there in
Such a short time,
And to renew old
Acquaintances that have
Survived the night.

Struggling in the droppings
Of a million rats and
Grasping the empty bottles
That have served as
Passports to their paradise,
They gaze with dead black
Eyes upon a world that does not
Know them.

The tower of gold that
Beckons in the cold
Afternoon and shines
Upon the skinless skeletons
Who mumble about success
And scorn failure and those
Who have failed,
Only to realize that they
Missed finding out
What the hell it was all about.

The maggots and the roaches
Devour the remains of the
Heroes and delight in
The body juices that
Flow freely from the
Broken spirits of those
Who weep for someone else.

And so ends another happy day.

Through an Amber Glass

Somehow
I cannot see you
As clearly
As once I could

Somehow
I cannot feel the same
Although I
Wish I could

Sometimes
Though the pain is great
There is
No comfort here

Sometimes
When I am lonely
On cold nights
Memories comfort me

Always
Through this amber glass
I never see
I never feel
There is no comfort

But
    No
        One
           Hears
                Me
                    Cry.

Time and Memories

Fallen heroes
Rise up from the dust,
As dreams play through
The mists.
Memories that take forever
To shed their masks,
As the rain that beats
Against the window
Slowly fades.
This way again, pass this
Way again and let time
Wear a smile and leave me
With a tender moment's
Thought.

Time, Roads, Circles

Every person is an island.
No amount of love
Or caring
Can span the gap between
Us, save for a few
Moments.

And even then, it is a
Tenuous bridge,
A spider's strand,
Broken by time and
Our inability to
Give of ourselves totally
And completely;
For we know that
Our lives are
Preordained, destined to
End without flowers,
Leaving only a stray
Thought, a wisp of
Remembrance as other lives
Go on.

Although I understand this,
I struggle to avoid
The fate
That lies in wait
For all of us.

Tonight

And when I'm not with you
I feel an emptiness inside that no
Amount of whiskey or cheap love can erase;
I think myself a fool for feeling
This way, and knowing that
It is all for naught.
If only we could laugh again
And skip stones
Peacock blue across the water
And dream our dreams again,
Hot summers and high tides;
And the songs we knew, oh God,
The songs we knew,
And the things we've been
Oh, God the things we've been...
Just memories,
Sweet memories,
Tonight.

I stand to listen and
Hear nothing;
I reach to touch and
Feel naught;
There is void, absence of light
And yet my eyes seek
To flee and fly the prison
And behold others as they gaze upon
The monument;
Fascinated, their hands
Claw the walls and their
Cries are borne into the night
And disappear;
For I am one with the stone,
Alone on this windswept plain,
Distant from the horizon.

Within

Silence,
A soft pervasive
Absence of sound and feeling;
Loneliness,
A state of non-being,
Hoping to give and to share,
Yet only the desert
Greets the thirsty man,
Only the sun beats down
Upon the parched mind,
Seeking sound, searching
For a way to laugh
Around the tears.
Forgotten,
The souls we knew
And never knew,
Perhaps only glimpsed
Through our blindness;
And we are all the
Same,
Within ourselves.

You

You cast the light upon my darkness,
And send the waves to roll upon my shores
With tenderness.

I am humble in my thanks
For all the moments softly fading,
Sunsets that dissolve into
The mists, a cat's paw haze.

I may draw the shade against the night,
Ne'er against my feelings
For you.

My Heart Was Fallow Ground

My heart was fallow ground
And had been that way for years,
Never having good seeds sown
And watered only by my tears.

Then the day arrived
When all of that would change,
As I became aware at last
That I could shed those awful chains.

The gloom then started to recede
And I travelled toward the light,
Finding truth with open eyes
Joyous in my new-found sight.

Awaiting me was a treasure trove
Of riches beyond compare,
And I found myself immersed in love
With a lovely lady fair.

I grew to love her like none before
As we began our cautious walk,
The laughter came so easily
As did our endless talk.

We pledged our vows straight from the heart
And settled into life.
I, her loving husband,
And she, my loving wife.

Many years have passed since then
With joy and tears we shared,
And through it all we now give thanks
To God who put us there.

For there is no doubt that it was He
Who crafted such a bond,
Of two souls drifting on the tide
In search of love so very long.

Now here we are in our golden years
With memories galore,
And the talk and laughter still remain
And we want for nothing more.

This life was good in many ways
And those memories do bring smiles,
As we recount the passing years
And life's enchanting miles.

We owe our fortune to God above
Who helped us find the way,
Our lives were guided by His hand
And our love prevails today.

This Stormy Sea

We sail upon this stormy sea,
No port in sight for you and me.
Our souls are tattered, torn and frayed
Perhaps on shore we should have stayed.

But then again it matters not,
To learn a lesson time forgot.
And chart a course so preordained,
To venture forth on bounding main.

To face the storm and bravely stand
Against the wind to hold command;
As stalwart sailors we shall be
Without the answers, you and me.

But hazards seem to come and go,
We hold our course first fast, then slow;
And try to keep a steady helm
As miles define this finite realm.

We search for peace as time goes by,
Fair winds, calm seas and cloudless skies,
Through toil and storm, we trim our sails
As many expectations fail.

Then comes the time to navigate
Through rocky shoals and windy straits
No lighthouse there to light the way
As night begins to have its say.

And far away the lights are seen
Of our safe harbor like our dreams,
Then nearer yet we sail so free,
Against the wind, both you and me.

The last horizon draws so near,
As we begin to taste the fear.
Yet onward is our destiny
That waits for us, both you and me.

The final inlet must be sailed
By those of us who have not failed
To seek our one and only home,
Alas, it must be sailed alone.

Sandi

I sat alone on a windswept shore,
The cry of gulls my company,
And gazed upon the ocean, there
I saw your eyes look back at me.

The sound of waves at endless toil,
Did break into my reverie,
As thoughts of you on daydream wings
Carried your laughter back to me.

The touch of sea so close at hand,
The reach of sky so far above,
Are wondrous, yet they still remain
A shade of grey without your love.

Serenity

Here am I on bended knee
Just this side of eternity
Thanking God for how I've grown
And all the things I've ever known.

The smell of coffee is a comfort borne
On the chilly air of a frosty morn,
It brings me to a place of calm
And soothes my soul like a healing balm.

I love the feeling from the first good taste
And not a drop will go to waste,
Like nectar from a tender bloom
This bitter brew that sheds the gloom.

Then I gaze upon the day
With all my worries far away,
The world so new, serene and still
The silence soon will slowly fill

With the songs of birds that now take wing,
And a breeze that will surely bring
A melody of life and love
To welcome ears and skies above.

The sun is peeking from a pastel sky,
Gaining courage as the clouds drift by
And casts its light in golden hues
Through pinks and orange and violet blues.

The gentle waves caress the shore
As they will forever more
And time stands still for all to see
The beauty and tranquility.

I walk the sands of endless time,
And for a moment that is sublime
The shore, beyond my wildest dreams
Is mine alone, or so it seems.

But there my journey will not end,
For Autumn is just around the bend
With colored chaos that makes one sigh,
Glory unfolding before one's eyes.

With the crackle of leaves as company,
Like a joyous, noisy symphony,
My steps are light but somehow bold,
Crushing copper, maize, red and gold.

I wander with no destination,
Content with feeling all sensations,
Moments residing in my heart,
I've loved them all right from the start.

I hope my travels never end,
But time can't be a longtime friend
I feel a peace that I have to share
With all my friends it's only fair.

My fervent wish is that you find
Your life well-lived, indeed sublime.
And precious moments, may they be
Gift-wrapped in serenity.

About the Author

The author is located in Midland, Georgia. He lives there with his wife of over forty years, Sandi. They are homebodies who are enjoying their retirement years together.